# VITAL BEGINNINGS

## Your New Life in Christ

TIM GREEN

Barefoot Ministries
Kansas City, MO

ISBN 083-415-0034

Printed in the United States of America
Editor: James K. Hampton
Cover Design: Paul Franitza



10 9 8 7 6 5 4 3 2 1

# TABLE OF CONTENTS

# 1 What Happened?—God's Grace, Our Faith

## Real Life

What an incredible youth meeting! Andrea had been attending the activities for teens at this church for a while now, but this particular service was awesome. At the end of the worship service, the youth leader, Pastor Jon, asked if anyone would like to receive the Lord as their Savior. Andrea didn't quite understand everything that was going on, but she had heard enough about God's love and forgiveness that she raised her hand and she prayed a simple prayer. Andrea knew that something awesome had taken place. But what—what happened?

For four days now, Andrea had been waiting. Finally, tonight she would be meeting with six other people—some who had been on the Christian journey for a while and others who, like her, had just begun this journey. She couldn't wait to get with the group and find out more about what it meant to *be* a Christian.

As her group of six got together, they each shared about their lives over the last several days. They shared both their ups and their downs. They then prayed for each other and for other needs in their youth group. After prayer, Pastor Jon said, "Tonight we are going to explore just what it means to *become* a Christian. In the Bible, there is a collection of letters from a man named Paul. As Christians would gather together just like we've gathered tonight, they would anticipate receiving letters from Paul. In these letters, Paul would answer questions that they had—in fact many of the same questions that all of us have asked: What happened to us? What's happening to us now? What does it mean to have become a 'Christian?' What does it mean to *be* a Christian?

"There are a couple of words that are repeated several times in the Bible that we need to properly understand before we proceed. Paul speaks about having *'righteousness.'* This word actually means 'right-relatedness.' In other words, to be righteous is to have a right relationship with God and with other people. The other word Paul uses is *'justify.'* This word is closely related to righteousness; it simply means 'to put someone in a right relationship with someone else' or 'to make righteous.'"

## Dialogue with Scripture

Pastor Jon began to lead the members of the group through a Bible study to help them find the answers to the questions they had. Following is the handout Pastor Jon led them through. As you work through it, keep in mind the definitions of "righteousness" and "justify."

The first letter that we are going to explore is the letter to the Ephesians. Read Ephesians 2:1-10. In the first three verses, Paul describes where all of us were before we began to follow Jesus.

**1.** In verse 1, what does Paul say has made us like dead people?

**2.** According to verse 3, how do those who are dead in their sins live?

In verses 4-10, Paul describes where we are now that we are followers of Jesus and what He calls us to do.

**3.** According to verses 4-6, what did God do while we were dead because of our sins?

**4.** According to verse 4, what is it about God that caused Him to give us life?

**5.** It is God who acted first to save us. What word does Paul use in verse 5 to describe how we have been saved?

**6.** According to verse 8, since we have been given life (saved) by grace, it is not from ____________ own doing, but it is the gift of ________________.

**7.** According to verse 9, since the relationship we have with God is not the result of our own accomplishments, no one can __________________.

To get even a better picture of what it means to have a relationship with God because of grace, read Romans 5:6-11.

**8.** According to verse 6, while we were totally helpless and could do nothing to give life to ourselves, what did Christ do?

**9.** According to verse 8, God demonstrates His love for all of us by Christ's __________________ for us while we were still _______________________.

**10.** According to verse 11, who is responsible for reconciling us (putting us back into a right relationship) with God?

So if the relationship we have with God is about what He has done (grace) and not what we have done (works), then what part do we play? Read what Paul says about our response to grace, first in Romans 5:1.

**11.** According to Romans 5:1, we have been justified (put into a right relationship) through what?

Now read Philippians 3:4-11 where Paul talks about our response to grace—faith. Here we discover what it means to have a relationship with Christ based upon *faith* rather than upon what we can accomplish in our own strength.

**12.** In verses 4-6, what are some of Paul's religious accomplishments that he describes?

**13.** In verses 7-8, how does Paul view these accomplishments now?

**14.** Rather than a life of accomplishments and personal achievements, what does Paul say, in verses 8 and 10, is now his goal?

**15.** According to verse 9, the right relationship (righteousness) we have is not based on our own righteousness that comes from the ______________, but rather a right relationship (righteousness) that comes from ___________________ and is by __________________.

**16.** So what has happened to us? Because the right relationship we now have with God and other people is based on what God has done, we are saved (given life) by God's ______________. Our response is ___________________ or simply trusting that God's grace is enough to give us life!

### Scripture Memorization

***For it is by grace you have been saved, through faith—and this not from yourselves, it is the gift of God—not by works, so that no one can boast.***

**—Ephesians 2:8-9**

## Where Am I?

If someone were to ask me what has God done in my life, how would I respond?

What does it mean for my life to not only be saved by grace but to keep living every moment by grace?

What does it mean for my life to not only have trusted God in the past to give me life, but for me to live each moment of this spiritual journey trusting God to keep giving me life?

## Sharing the Journey

- Spend some time with your mentor sharing how your journey with Christ has gone this week.
- Discuss with your mentor what being saved by grace means for your life right now. Share also with your mentor how you are responding to God's grace by trust or faith.
- Since our response to receiving a gift should be gratitude, share in a thanksgiving prayer with your mentor in which you both express thanks to God for His grace in the past, today, and in the journey ahead.

# 2 On the Journey

## Real Life

What a week! Although she was really busy, Andrea had been looking forward all week to getting back with her accountability group to share what all had happened. She had learned so much about this life of God's grace and our faith last week that she couldn't wait to see what she would discover tonight.

After the group opened with a prayer, they began to share what their week had been like, both the "high points" and "low points." Andrea was amazed at how each person's reflections, while different, were so much alike—especially what Brandon shared. Brandon explained to the group that last week he had done great. But this week had been so different. He had really struggled with staying consistent in his journey with God throughout the week, and the emotional high that he had been on for several days just hadn't lasted! Brandon exclaimed, "I thought I had it all together; I wonder now if I have anything at all!" It seemed that everybody in the group could identify with what Brandon was saying.

Even Pastor Jon said that he could identify. However, he then went on to remind the group that what they had learned last week was that when Jesus forgives us of our sins that we are then in a "right relationship" with God and with others. Pastor Jon explained: "But relationships are ongoing; they are dynamic. We don't just enter into a relationship with someone, get our 'relationship card' stamped and then stop! Relationships continue; they grow and develop. That's the way it is in our relationship with God as well.

"One of the biggest misunderstandings that we often have is seeing Jesus as a 'quick fix' to life's problems, temptations, and struggles. But Jesus is not a quick fix; He is a lifelong partner. The Christian life is not just getting somewhere and stopping; it is a journey."

Pastor Jon then compared it to when your family pulls out of the driveway; they've made a very important decision to get on the road and start a trip, but the trip has just begun! In the same way, each of us are on a journey, a lifelong journey with God—but it's just started. What now lies ahead is an incredible adventure!

## Dialogue with Scripture

Following is the handout that Andrea's group worked through that night. Read and answer each of the questions.

The scriptures that we are going to look at talk a lot about the Christian life being a journey.

1. Read Philippians 3:12-16. What does Paul say in verses 12 and 13 about having already arrived?

2. In verse 12, rather than having already obtained the goal, Paul says that he does what?

3. According to verse 13 what two things does Paul do to continue in the journey? ___________________ what is behind, and ____________________ toward what is ahead.

4. Now read Hebrews 12:1-2. According to verse 1, what are we to throw off in order to make the journey?

5. As we run the race, on whom are we to keep our eyes?

So if we have not "arrived" at some destination but are on an adventure-filled journey with God, how do we live in this journey? In order to discover how the daily walk takes place, read 1 John 1:5-2:2.

6. How does verse 5 describe God?

**7.** What does it mean for us to "walk in darkness" (verse 6)?

**8.** According to verses 5 and 6, why is not possible to "walk in darkness" and at the same time have a good relationship (fellowship) with God?

**9.** According to verse 7, if we walk in light rather than darkness, there are two things that continually take place in our lives: we have ____________________ with one another and the blood of Jesus continually cleanses us from all ________________.

Verses 8-10 of chapter 1 and the first verse of chapter 2 describe what we do with sin (darkness) in our lives. Read these verses once again.

**10.** According to the first verse of chapter 2, the purpose of this letter is so that we will not do what?

**11.** According to verse 1, if we do sin, who is our advocate or the One to whom we can go with our sin?

**12.** According to 1:9, when we come to Christ with our sin, what are we to do?

**13.** According to verse 9, when we confess or admit our sin, Christ is faithful and He will do what?

a) Forgive us our ____________________;

b) Purify us from all ____________________________ (broken relationship).

**14.** What do verses 8 and 10 tell us about "covering up" our sins?

## Scripture Memorization

***But if we walk in the light, as he is in the light, we have fellowship with one another, and the blood of Jesus, his Son, purifies us from all sin.***

**—1 John 1:7**

As this week's accountability group meeting came to an end, each person shared their hopes for the journey this coming week. Pastor Jon challenged them to remain totally open and honest with God throughout the week. He shared that people on a journey are committed to the long haul, not just quick fixes. He said that on the journey there will be temptations to get off the track, but temptations to get off the track are not the same thing as getting off the track. And Jesus will give us all the grace and help we need to face the temptation.

As the group joined hands and prayed for each other, the time came for Brandon to pray. His prayer was brief and to the point: "God, keep us on the journey; keep us in the light; keep us honest. No cover-ups! Amen."

## Where Am I?

As I continue on this journey, what things of the past is God inviting me to leave behind?

Over the past week, how have I been dealing with temptation when it comes?

In my journey with God, what makes it most difficult for me to be honest and open with God? How can I develop honesty with God?

As I look to what is ahead, what will it mean to keep my eyes on Jesus, "the author and perfecter" of my faith?

## Sharing the Journey

Share with your mentor how your journey has been this week. What were some significant "mile markers" or celebrations in the journey? What were some significant difficulties along the path?

# 3 Participating in the Family—the Body of Christ

## Real Life

Only a few days had passed since Brandon's accountability group last met, but it already seemed like weeks! He kept reflecting on what the group had talked about last week—that the relationship we have with Christ is a journey. However, to Brandon, it seemed like he had put on his spiritual backpack and was making the journey all alone. Particularly this week, he felt as if he were the only one at school, at his job, even at home that really cared about an ongoing journey with God. Several times during the week, he had imagined himself as a lone hiker, facing the challenges and dangers of a steep mountain all by himself. He knew that God would be faithful, but it sure would help if a few other people were making the hike with him!

Finally the longest seven days of his life had passed. Brandon couldn't wait to get back with his accountability group. In the group, Brandon described how, even though he knew that God had been with him all week, he felt so "by himself." Several others in the group shared the same feeling. Pastor Jon responded, "That's funny you brought this up, Brandon. Tonight we're going to talk exactly about what you're facing. Last week, we talked about the journey we make with God. But tonight, we're going to talk about the journey we make with other people."

Pastor Jon explained that to be on the journey with Jesus means that we are a part of something a whole lot bigger than just us. "As we're journeying with Christ, it's never just 'me and Jesus.' It's always me, Jesus, and a whole lot of other people. We are a part of a family that stretches across countries, languages, and cultures."

Let's pause a moment before Pastor Jon continues. Can you think of a story or two about Christians in another part of the world that you have heard recently? Perhaps a missionary in a foreign country, or a Christian who was persecuted for their faith?

Pastor Jon continued. "We are also a part of a family that stretches across time. This family isn't made up just of people who are alive today but of the millions who made the journey before us."

Can you think of three people who made this journey before you?

## Dialogue with Scripture

Following is the handout that Brandon's group worked through that night. Read and answer each of the questions.

This week we're examining just what it means for us to participate in this family of God.

Read 1 Corinthians 12:12-27.

**1.** To what does Paul compare the family of God?

**2.** Describe how this comparison shows that we are a part of something bigger than just ourselves.

**3.** According to verses 12, 13, and 20 how many "bodies" of Jesus are there?

**4.** What does this say to us about God's family to which we belong?

**5.** According to verses 12, 14, and 20 how many "parts" of the body are there?

6. What does this say to us about God's family to which we belong?

7. Look at verses 14-17 again. What happens if a part of the body, such as the foot, feels inferior to another part of the body, such as the hand, and decides that it doesn't belong to the body?

8. What does this say to those of us that feel inferior to other members of the Body of Christ?

9. According to verse 17, what would happen to the human body if the whole body were just one body part?

10. What would happen to the Body of Christ if the whole Body were just one body part?

**11.** According to verses 21-25, what happens if a part of the body, such as the eye, thinks that it could be the body on its own and would tell the hand, "I don't need you?"

**12.** What does this say to those of us that feel like we can make the journey by ourselves?

**13.** Read verses 25 and 26. If one part of the body suffers, what do the rest of the body parts do? If one part of the body celebrates, what do the rest of the body parts do?

**14.** What difference does it make that in verse 27, when Paul says YOU are the Body of Christ, he is not talking to just one person but to a group of people?

## Scripture Memorization

***The body is a unit, though it is made up of many parts; and though all its parts are many, they form one body. So it is with Christ . . . Now you are the body of Christ, and each one of you is a part of it.***

**—1 Corinthians 12:12, 27**

## Where Am I?

How do I deal with people in the Body of Christ who are different than me?

Who are five people that I know in the Body of Christ, and what are their contributions to the Body?

What do I contribute to the Body of Christ?

## Sharing the Journey

- Share with your mentor how you have been relating to the Body of Christ over the past few weeks. When do you feel most like you are making the journey alone? Do you feel inferior? Do you feel that you can make it by yourself?
- Discuss with your mentor, how you can best find your place within the Body of Christ that you are a part of.
- An important part of being in the Body of Christ is finding a person or group with whom we can be accountable. Discuss with your mentor how you are doing with accountability.

# 4 Spending Time in the Family Album

## Real Life

Andrea had been looking forward to tonight's group meeting all week. For four weeks now, she had been reading this special book Pastor Jon had given her, studying it, even memorizing parts of it. She had many friends who had copies of the book, but what in the world was it? She had to admit that it really did have some cool stories in it, but it also had some things in it that, to be honest, were very tough to make sense of.

*So what is this book called "The Bible"?* Andrea wondered. *How is a person supposed to use it? What makes it any different than any other book?* These questions had been bugging her for some time, so that was the reason for her excitement about tonight's meeting. She knew that her group was going to be discussing the Bible—what it is, why it's important, and how we should use it.

As soon as the group all arrived, Pastor Jon reminded them what they had discussed last week—that we are a part of something so much bigger than ourselves, a family, the body of Jesus. Then as a family, they all shared how their journey had gone during the week and they prayed for each other.

After prayer, Pastor Jon talked about another important part of belonging to a family. "My great-grandmother collected family pictures and souvenirs ever since she was a little girl. In addition, she wrote down stories about family events. My grandfather did the same, sometimes even writing poems and songs about our family. My mother saves letters. She saved all the letters that my dad wrote to her when they were dating as well as the ones I wrote to her when I was in college."

Pastor Jon passed around the group some scrapbooks filled with pictures, mementos, family stories, poems, and letters. He said, "A lot of times, I just like to kick back and go through these scrapbooks. When I do, I rediscover who I am, where I came from, and what kind of things are really important to me and my family." Then he said something that stuck with everybody in the group: "The family of God has an incredible scrapbook as well. It's full of stories, poems, songs, and letters by our ancestors about their journey with God. It's called the Bible."

## Dialogue with Scripture

Following is the handout that Andrea's group worked through that night. Read and answer each of the questions.

The book of Hebrews was written for a group of Christians who were going through some pretty tough times in the journey. Some even thought about giving up.

**1.** Look at the first two verses of chapter 12. What does the writer encourage these Christians to do?

a)__________ __________ everything that hinders and the sin that so easily entangles;

b) ______________ with perseverance the race marked out for us;

c) ________ ________ __________ on Jesus, "the author and perfecter of our faith."

It's important to note that before the encouragement to keep on the journey is ever given in verses 1-2, the author gives us the reason behind the encouragement."

**2.** In verse 1, the motivation for Jesus' followers to keep running the race is that we are surrounded by a great cloud of ________________.

So who are these "witnesses"? They are those women and men who made the same journey that we're now making. In chapter eleven of Hebrews, many of our ancestors who have already run the race are described.

**3.** Read through chapter eleven, and describe three of these witnesses that especially speak to where you are in the journey right now.

(1)

(2)

(3)

This "cloud of witnesses" that encourages us in the journey is not only found in this one chapter of the Bible. In fact, this chapter is like a snapshot of what the entire Bible is about. As we open up our family album—the Bible—we are reminded over and over again that we really do belong to an incredible family—the family of God. This family has passed on its scrapbook filled with snapshots, stories, mementos, poems, songs, and letters. Reading the Bible really is like getting into our family scrapbook and finding out where we came from, who our ancestors are, and what makes us who we are!

The Bible, our Christian family scrapbook, is made up of all sorts of materials. Spend some time looking at some of these different materials and reflecting on what it says to you about your being a member of the family of God:

**4.** Many times we hear stories of the journey that our ancestors made with God—with all of its ups and downs. Read two brief stories found in 1 Samuel 17:38-49 and Luke 15:1-7 and write down a statement of what it says about belonging to the family of God.

5. Sometimes we hear sermons that our ancestors preached about God. Look at one brief sermon found in Micah 6:6-8 and write down a statement regarding what it says about belonging to the family of God.

6. Sometimes we hear songs and prayers that our ancestors sang and prayed when they came together for worship. Look at one brief song as found in Psalm 146 and write down what it says about belonging to the family of God.

7. Sometimes we read letters that were written to our ancestors about the journey they were making with God. Read a portion of one of those letters found in 1 Timothy 2:1-7 and write down what it says about belonging to the family of God.

Not only does the Bible gives us snapshots, memories, and stories of our ancestors, but like a good family scrapbook should do, it lets us know what it means to belong to the family of God! Paul wrote a letter to Timothy in which Paul describes how the Bible works in our lives. Read a section of that letter in 2 Timothy 3:16-17.

**8.** What are four ways in which Paul describes the use of the Bible:

(1) (3)

(2) (4)

## Scripture Memorization

***All scripture is inspired by God and is useful for teaching, for reproof, for correction, and for training in righteousness, so that everyone who belongs to God may be proficient, equipped for every good work.***

**—2 Timothy 3:16-17**

## Where Am I?

How have certain stories in the Bible already given me insight into what it means to belong to God's family?

How consistent am I in reading the Bible?

What are the obstacles that I might face that could prevent me from consistently reading the Bible?

## Sharing the Journey

- Share with your mentor a regular plan of Bible reading, perhaps starting with a particular book of the Bible.
- Discuss with your mentor any questions that you may be having right now about what the Bible is, how you might use it as your Christian family album, and/or struggles that you have in reading the Bible.

# 5 Dialoging with God

## Real Life

Every week since the accountability group had begun meeting, they had started the same way—by praying together. The longer Justin was on the journey, the more he became curious about this prayer thing. Even though he joined everyone else and prayed, the whole thing was so odd to him. What was up with talking to someone you can't even see? What are you supposed to do when you pray? Is there a certain way to pray? For that matter, why even pray?

This week, as soon as the opening prayer was over, Justin exclaimed, "Okay, I've got to know—what's the deal with this prayer thing? What's it all about?" As soon as he asked the question, everyone else in the group was jumping in with the same kind of questions. Everybody seemed to pray, but nobody really knew what they were doing or why they were doing it.

That was all Pastor Jon needed. He responded, "Great questions! We've been sharing over the past several weeks about the journey that we're on—a journey with God and a journey with each other. This journey is all about a dynamic, growing, honest relationship. In any relationship that is honest and growing, conversations take place.

Sometimes they're long; at other times, they're only a few words. Sometimes they're a couple friends catching up on the latest news, sometimes they're one friend asking another friend to help out, and sometimes they're one friend patiently listening to what another friend is going through."

Pastor Jon went on to say that prayer is the conversation we share with God. "Just as any healthy and growing relationship has honest, ongoing conversation, the journey we share with God must have honest, ongoing conversation! Prayer is not only talking to God, but it is also listening to God. It is recognizing and responding to the incredible fact that the God who loves us and who is continually providing His grace to us is with us every moment of the journey. But what does a conversation with God look like?"

## Dialogue with Scripture

Following is the handout that Justin's group worked through that night. Read and answer each of the questions.

Our family album—the Bible—gives us some great examples of what a conversation with God looks like. Many of these prayers are found in the book of Psalms.

**1.** Look at the following parts of prayers in the Bible and describe what is going on in the conversation with God.

Psalm 9:1-2

Psalm 18:1-3

Psalm 51:1-4

Psalm 86:1-7

Now that we've looked at some examples of prayers in the Bible, let's discuss how to pray. By now you've had the opportunity to hear several different people pray. Perhaps you even have marveled that people like your pastor, Sunday School teacher, and even your mentor know exactly what kind of words to say when they pray. You may have even expressed this concern: "I'd like to pray, but how can I learn all the right words?" Well, the good news is that Jesus had something really important to say about "all the right words" in prayer. Look at Matthew 6:5-13.

**2.** According to verses 5-8, what seems to be most important in prayer?

After teaching that the most important thing in prayer is not "just saying the right words," Jesus goes on to show His disciples what prayer looks like by teaching them a prayer that we continue to pray today called the Lord's Prayer. At the very beginning of our prayer time, this prayer asks us to reflect on what God is like.

**3.** What kind of things do the opening lines, "Our Father in heaven, hallowed be your name" tell us about God?

Once we understand what God is like, we can then share our deepest concerns with God. In our journey with God, our deepest desire is what we have been celebrating over the past several weeks—that God really will "be God" in our lives; in other words that God's "kingdom come" among us.

**4.** According to verse 10, what does it mean for God's kingdom to come in our lives?

God's desire or will for our lives is that He really will "be God" in every area of our daily lives.

**5.** What are the three areas of our lives described in verses 11-13?

(1) (2) (3)

**6.** What does it mean to trust God "for our daily bread" (v. 11)?

**7.** What does it mean to trust God for forgiveness (v. 12)?

**8.** What does it mean trust God for protection (v. 13)?

## Scripture Memorization

***This, then, is how you should pray:***
***"Our Father in heaven, hallowed be your name, your kingdom come, your will be done, on earth as it is in heaven. Give us today our daily bread. Forgive us our debts as we also have forgiven our debtors. And lead us not into temptation, but deliver us from the evil one, for your is the kingdom and the power, and the glory forever. Amen."***

**—Matthew 6:9-13**

The time had gone so quickly in this week's meeting, but Justin still had so many questions about prayer. However, tonight he had come to realize just how important it was to have daily conversation with God as they journeyed together.

As the meeting came to an end, Pastor Jon explained that because prayer is a conversation, it should be a *dialogue*—in other words, we not only talk to God, but we also "listen" to God. This "listening" to God is not about hearing a voice or getting some type of emotional feeling.

Rather it's simply taking the time to stop doing all the talking and to allow God to assure us that He will provide our "daily bread," that He does forgive our sins, and that He will protect us along the journey. It may include reflecting on a verse of the Bible that we have read or sharing with an accountability partner or mentor.

This week, the group closed their time together with several minutes of quiet time, allowing God to assure them of His faithfulness, grace, and presence in their lives.

## Where Am I?

How has my daily conversation with God been going over the past week? What are the positive points? What struggles have I faced when I pray?

The best time of the day for me to have a concentrated time of prayer is. . .

Based upon my understanding of the prayer that Jesus taught His disciples in Matthew 6:9-13, in my own words that prayer sounds like this. . .

## Sharing the Journey

- Share with your mentor the questions or concerns that you have about prayer.
- Discuss with your mentor what she or he has discovered to be the best time of the day to have an extended time of prayer.
- As you have been listening to God, share with your mentor how God has recently been speaking in your life.
- Spend time with your mentor in prayer, both talking and listening to God.

# 6 Living in God's Presence

## Real Life

After five weeks together, the group had come to know each other well and had really begun to trust each other. Just like the weeks before, Pastor Jon invited the group to share how their journey had been over the past week. After a couple of students had reflected on their journey, Brandon shared with the group. "This has been an awesome week! Everything I read in the Bible this week just seemed to jump off the pages and come alive, and the dialogue I've had with God through prayer this week has been incredible. I've never had a week where I was just so sure that God was with me every step of the journey!"

Andrea wasn't sure if she should say anything, but then she decided that this group really was her Christian family and that she could be honest with them. So she jumped in, "I hate to give the other side of the picture, but my week has been just the opposite of Brandon's. I just haven't felt God at all! Whenever I would read the Bible, nothing made sense. When I prayed, it seemed that I was talking into thin air. Even when I tried to worship on Sunday at church, I just didn't feel a thing! I'm sorry everybody, but I just didn't feel God with me on the journey this week at all!"

For a few seconds, everybody in the room was quiet, until Pastor Jon said, "Thanks Andrea. Thanks for your honesty. You don't need to apologize to any of us. In fact, tonight we're going to explore a little more what you're talking about. What does it mean for us to live in God's presence—every step of the journey—even when we might *feel* like God is nowhere to be found?"

Pastor Jon asked if anyone else in the group had ever felt the way Andrea described. Several other people described times when they too didn't *feel* God's presence. Pastor Jon said, "You're not the first people to *feel* this way. In fact, the book of Psalms gives us several examples of people who wondered where God was. Let's look at them now."

## Dialogue with Scripture

Following is the handout that Andrea's group worked through that night. Read and answer each of the questions.

Let's look at three prayers in the book of Psalms where people wondered where God was. What's going on in the life of the person praying each prayer that might make the person *feel* like God is absent?

Psalm 42:1-3 and 9-11

Psalm 102:1-4

Psalm 109:1-5

Sometimes when we're going through rough times, when we're physically sick or tired, when our relationships are not going well, or when we might just be "feeling down," we might also begin to *feel* that God isn't with us. However, God's presence with us is never determined by the situation we're in nor is it determined by how we're feeling. God's presence is a fact—not a feeling! God's presence is a promise He makes—not something we work to get! God's presence, just like God's grace, is a gift with which God provides us!

Let's look at three stories where God's presence is a matter of fact and a promise from God: Exodus 3:1-12; Jeremiah 1:4-8; Mark 4:35-41.

**1.** In the story in Exodus 3, what has been happening to God's people according to verse 7?

**2.** In light of what has been going on, in verse 10 God asks Moses to go to ____________________ to bring God's people out of ____________________.

**3.** When Moses hears what God wants him to do, he re-

sponds to God in verse 11 with these words: ________
________ ________ that I should go to Pharaoh?"

**4.** When Moses is concerned about what will equip him to do the job, God's promise to Moses in verse 12 is that "I will be ________ ________."

**5.** In Jeremiah 1:5, what does God say that He has appointed Jeremiah to be? ________________________

________________

**6.** When Jeremiah hears this call from God, his response in verse 6 is "I do not know how to ________________; I am only a ____________."

**7.** When Jeremiah is concerned about how he will be able to do the job that God has asked him to do, what does God promise him in verse 8? "Do not be ____________ of them, for I am ________ ________ and will rescue you."

**8.** In Mark 4, what happened to the disciples when they were on the lake in v. 37?

**9.** When the disciples thought they were going to drown (even though Jesus was also in the boat with them during the storm), note how they expressed their *feelings* in verse 38: "Teacher, don't ________ ________ if we drown?"

**10.** After Jesus calmed the storm, His response to the disciples in v. 40 was, "Why are you so ___________? Do you still have no _________________?"

In all three of these stories, even when the situation faced or the emotions felt seemed to point to something different, God's presence was a fact!

Now we are going to "practice the presence" of Christ. Since God's promise never to leave us or abandon us is a fact, rather than focusing on the situation we are facing or the *feelings* that we are having, we should focus on what this God who is with us is like. "Focus on God"—what a great idea!

**11.** Read the following four passages that describe God. After you read each one, write one word that summarizes what the passage says God is like.

Psalm 103:8-13

Isaiah 40:29-31

Ezekiel 34:11-16

Romans 3:31-39

**12.** Can you think of three songs that describe what God is like? Write one word that summarizes what God is like in each song.

(1)

(2)

(3)

## Scripture Memorization

***Be strong and courageous. Do not be terrified; do not be discouraged, for the LORD your God will be with you wherever you go.***

**—Joshua 1:9**

Before the group was dismissed, Andrea exclaimed: "Thanks everybody! My whole focus is changing. It's not the emotions I have. It's not whether things are going good or bad. It's not even whether I am feeling excited or feeling tired. Rather it's all about the God who has promised to be with us. He's my focus; my trust is in Him!" With that new focus, Andrea and the rest of the group were ready to continue the journey.

## Where Am I?

At what times do I most sense God's presence? At what times do I seem most to question God's presence?

In what ways does my devotional life of prayer and Bible reading enable me to practice the presence of Christ?

In what ways do the various parts of the worship service enable me to practice the presence of Christ?

Scripture reading

hymns and choruses

prayer

the pastor's sermon

the taking of Holy Communion

In what ways does my gathering with an accountability group or my mentor enable me to practice the presence of Christ?

## Sharing the Journey

- Discuss with your mentor when you most sense God's presence and when you are most likely to question God's presence.
- Discuss with your mentor the significance of God's presence in our lives being a fact rather than a feeling or being dependent upon the situations we face.

Spend time with your mentor "practicing the presence" of Christ. Share with each other characteristics of God that you have discovered along the journey.

# 7 Called to Wholeness

## Real Life

Brandon just couldn't get out of his mind what Andrea had said at the end of last week's meeting: "God is my focus; my trust is in Him." All week, he kept thinking, "I do trust God, but on the other hand . . . well. . . ." He didn't know quite how to put into words what he was thinking. He just knew that he was on an incredible journey with God, but at the same time God seemed to be calling him to something deeper in this relationship. But what was it?

Brandon shared with his Bible study group what he had been thinking throughout the week. To Brandon's surprise, he was not alone. Others in the group were having the same thoughts. Pastor Jon reminded Brandon that to be on a journey means that we don't finally "arrive" at a place in our relationship with God and stop. "In fact," Pastor Jon continued, "I'd be worried if you didn't sense that God was calling you into a deeper walk with Him." But what? To what was God calling Brandon and the others with whom he was traveling?

## Dialogue with Scripture

Following is the handout that Brandon's group worked through that night. Read and answer each of the questions.

We need to remind ourselves where we began six weeks ago. Just so you don't forget, look again at Ephesians 2:8-9.

1. According to verse 8, our relationship with God is based upon the fact that "it is by ________________ we have been saved, through ______________________."

2. After having been on the journey this long, how would you define grace in your own words?

3. How would you define faith in your own words?

4. According to verses 8 and 9, being saved by God's grace is the opposite of what?

Here's the problem. Our being saved by God's free gift of grace and not by our own accomplishments or achievements is not just a one-time thing in the past. Every moment of every day in this journey, we receive life totally as a gift of God's grace. In response, we are called to live every moment of every day by faith or trust in God's grace.

While there are many passages in the Bible that express this call to live in a wholly trusting/loving response to God, the best summary of this call is in Jesus' words in what is often called the Greatest Commandment.

**5.** According to Mark 12:30, the call Jesus asks us to follow is that we should "____________ the Lord your God with __________ your heart and with __________ your soul and with ________________ your mind, and with ______________ your strength."

This call from God could be called *undivided trust* or even *perfect (whole) love.*

Perhaps you've been wondering about this trust issue. Maybe you've even said something like the following: "I trust God; I really have been responding to His grace with loving trust! But at the same time, I've gotten so used to trusting my own accomplishments and achievements—my grades, my athletic successes, my job, my friendships, even the religious stuff that I do. Sometimes I feel so divided. On one hand, I know that God's grace is enough to keep giving me life; on the other hand, I think that if I can do just the right things for myself, my family, my friends, and even for God then I'll *really* have life!"

If you've felt this way, then hear these four simple words of comfort: "Welcome to the family!" Throughout our family story, our ancestors struggled with this divided allegiance; however, God has continued to call us to love Him wholly—to trust Him undividedly. Let's take a closer look at this call.

Read Joshua 24:13-15. In these verses Joshua, the leader of the Israelites, calls the people (and us) to serve the Lord wholeheartedly.

**6.** Why is it important that Joshua first tells what God has done before calling the people to serve the Lord?

**7.** How does verse 13 demonstrate God's grace rather than human accomplishments?

**8.** In response to God's grace as demonstrated in verse 13, Joshua challenges the people of God in verse 14 to serve the Lord with _______ ____________________.

**9.** In order to serve the Lord wholly or undividedly, the people had to throw away the ___________ their forefathers worshipped. What does this mean for us?

Let's look at another challenge to this undivided trust in God. Look at 1 Kings 18:20-21. In this story, the prophet Elijah asks a question and then makes a challenge.

**10.** First, Elijah asks this question: "How long will you ________________ between two ____________________?" Then, Elijah gives this challenge to the people: "If the LORD is ______________, __________________ him; but if Baal is ________________, ______________________ him."

Now let's look at the challenge that Jesus gives to His disciples. Read a part of Jesus' sermon in Matthew 6:24-34.

**11.** In verse 24, what does Jesus say about trying to live a life of "divided" loyalties?

**12.** In verses 25-32, what are some examples that Jesus gives of things we might spend our life worrying about accomplishing?

**13.** When it comes to the basic things of life, Jesus tells us in verse 31 that we shouldn't spend our life worrying about them. Why? Because "your ____________ ________________ knows that you need them" (verse 32).

**14.** So what do we do with this problem of divided loyalties? Look again at Jesus' preaching in verse 33. Jesus calls us to seek first ______ ______________.

In order to discover what is meant by "seeking the kingdom of God," think back to our study two weeks ago when we explored the prayer that Jesus taught His disciples in Matthew 6:9-13.

**15.** According to Matthew 6:10, for us to pray "your kingdom come" means that we are desiring for God's "____________ be done on _____________ as it is in ____________________."

Right about now you may be thinking, *Yeah, but this undivided trust thing seems easier said than done. What am I going to do about it?* You're right. Just as our ancestors struggled with divided loyalty, so do we! Even though they tried harder and harder to love God wholly and to trust Him completely, they discovered that on their own initiative and in their own strength they just couldn't do it! They were so used to thinking that life was up to them and their accomplishments, they even applied it to their walk with God.

So is there any hope? Can we ever love God with all our heart, soul, mind, and strength? Is it possible for us to trust God undividedly? What's the answer?

Fortunately for us, there is some awesome news! God's grace is incredibly optimistic. God doesn't just leave us hanging! What we can't do—God's grace that saves us in the first place can do. God not only can forgive our sins and put us into a right relationship with Him, but in our journey with Him, God can even change the way we think!"

**16.** Take a look at Romans 12:1-2. According to verse 2, we are changed or transformed by the renewing of our

________________.

**17.** According to 12:2, as God changes our minds, we will then be able to test and approve (in other words, we can know) God's __________.

**18.** If God is the One who is changing our minds, what is our role? According to verse 1 we are called to offer our "________________ as living ________________, holy and pleasing to God."

**19.** It's important to understand that even offering ourselves to God isn't about our own accomplishments. According to verse 1, our offering ourselves to God is in response to God's ____________.

### Scripture Memorization

***I urge you, brothers, in view of God's mercy, to offer your bodies as living sacrifices, holy and pleasing to God—this is your spiritual act of worship. Do not conform any longer to the pattern of this world, but be transformed by the renewing of your mind.***

**—Romans 12:1-2a**

## Where Am I?

As I think about this journey I am on with Christ, I recognize that I struggle with "divided loyalties" in the following areas of my life:

In what ways do I sense that God is now calling me to a deeper walk with Him?

## Sharing the Journey

- Share with your mentor where you have seen divided loyalties in your journey. Work together to develop a plan to help you keep your focus on God's grace rather than your own accomplishments.
- Discuss with your mentor what it means to offer your body as a living sacrifice, holy and acceptable to God.
- Discuss with your mentor what is meant by the phrase "God's grace is very optimistic!"

# 8 Sharing God's Grace

## Real Life

Andrea couldn't believe that two months had already gone by since her Bible study group first started meeting together. During these two months, she had grown so much in her journey, and she knew that the journey ahead would be incredible. Tonight would be the final time that the group would get together; however, Andrea had joined a group of four other people just a couple weeks earlier for a weekly time of prayer, sharing, and accountability. Although she loved her new accountability group, she was going to miss meeting with this group with whom she had made these beginning steps. As Andrea arrived, she noticed that everybody else had similar feelings.

After the group prayed together, Pastor Jon asked a very straightforward question: "So, where do we go from here?" Several people tried to give him the answer they thought he was looking for, but he kept repeating the question: "Where do we go from here?" Finally, Brandon exclaimed, "What do you mean?" In response, Pastor Jon said something that the group would never forget.

"Seven weeks ago, we began to learn together what it means for us to receive God's grace and to live by that grace. But receiving grace is just the beginning! People who receive grace and forgiveness and love are called to become givers of grace and forgiveness and love. Tonight we're going to take a look at the awesome call that God is giving to us—a call for us now to move beyond being simply grace receivers and to become also grace givers."

## Dialogue with Scripture

Following is the handout that Andrea's group worked through that night. Read and answer each of the questions.

Jesus was a great storyteller. Read the story that He tells in Luke 15.1-7. In order to understand why Jesus tells this story, look back at verses 1 and 2.

1. What type of people were hanging out with Jesus in verse 1?

2. Why does the religious crowd, the Pharisees and the teachers of the law, get upset with Jesus in verse 2?

3. Why do you think the "religious insiders" (the teachers of the law and the Pharisees) think Jesus should not be with "religious outsiders" (the sinners and tax collectors)?

4. Look closely at verse 4. What doesn't seem to make sense about what the shepherd does with the other 99 sheep in this verse?

5. How does the shepherd react in verses 4 and 5 when he finds the lost sheep?

6. What would you say is the point to this story?

Take a look at a very similar story about Jesus in Mark 2:15-17.

7. What type of people was Jesus hanging out with this time?

**8.** In verses 16-17, the Pharisees and teachers of the law are concerned that Jesus is eating with these types of people. In response, Jesus answered, "It is not the _________________ who need a _________________, but the _______________. I have not come to call the _____________________, but sinners."

By now I hope you've realized just how much Jesus was a *grace giver!* To the outcasts, He gave acceptance; to the hurting, He brought peace; and to the lonely, He gave his presence. However, Jesus was not the only grace giver! He called those who journeyed with Him to become grace givers as well.

God is calling each of us to go beyond the places and people where we feel comfortable and to join Jesus, the Shepherd, in giving grace and forgiveness and love to confused, hurting, and lost sheep that are all around us.

So what does it look like for us to become grace givers at home, at school, at the job, and at church? Sharing the good news of God's free grace with others can take on many shapes. Throughout the Bible, we hear of many ways in which we can be grace givers to the people around us. Sometimes sharing God's grace takes the form of actions that we do; at other times, sharing God's grace takes the form of words that we say.

Much of the Bible encourages us to participate in simple actions of compassion for persons around us who are hurting or lonely.

**9.** Read Matthew 25:31-40. In verses 35-37, what six examples does Jesus give of giving grace to other people through *acts* of compassion?

(1) (4)

(2) (5)

(3) (6)

As we've discussed, sharing the grace of God with other people can also take the shape of the words that we speak to other people. Look at Ephesians 4:25-32.

**10.** According to verse 25, each of us are to put off ________________ and speak ________________. Rather than unwholesome words coming out of our mouths, verse 29 encourages us to speak only what is helpful for

____________________ ________________ __________.

**11.** In contrast to bitterness, anger, and slander, we give grace to others by being ________________ and ________________ to one another, ________________ each other, just as in Christ God forgave us (verse 32).

Then there are times when we become grace givers by simply sharing words with a friend or a family member of how God's grace has made a difference in our lives!

**12.** How would you briefly share with a friend what God has done and is doing in your life?

Whether through acts that we do or words that we say, the heart of grace giving is selfless love. God unselfishly has given us His love, and now we unselfishly share that love. In 1 Corinthians 13, we have an incredible picture of what love looks like.

**13.** Read verses 4-7. What are some of the descriptions of love in these verses?

Perhaps the greatest advice of how to be a young grace giver was given to another young person on the journey by his mentor, Paul.

**14.** In 1 Timothy 4:12, Paul encourages Timothy not to let anyone look down on him because he was ____________ but rather for Timothy to set an example for everyone else in his ____________, in his ________________, in his ________________, in his ________________ and in his ________________.

## Scripture Memorization

***When [Jesus] saw the crowds, he had compassion on them, because they were harassed and helpless, like sheep without a shepherd. Then he said to his disciples, "The harvest is plentiful but the workers are few. Ask the Lord of the harvest, therefore, to send out workers into his harvest field."***

**—Matthew 9:36-37**

## Where Am I?

How is God calling me to be a grace giver at my home? At my school? At my church?

What obstacles am I facing that are preventing me from being a grace giver?

What specific person in my life is God calling me to share grace and forgiveness?

## Sharing the Journey

It's important we live out the grace we have received. Share with your mentor what specific type of ministry God may be calling you to participate in so that you can be a grace giver.

- Discuss with your mentor how your church or youth group might become grace givers.
- As you now continue the journey, discuss with your mentor any particular questions or concerns that you are having.
- Share in a closing prayer with your mentor, thanking the Lord for His grace in your lives and asking the Lord to make both of you grace givers in the world in which you live.